Mandy

A trans woman's journey to Key West

Mandy Murray

'One Human Family - Unity Equality Diversity'
The motto of Key West
J T Thompson, 2000

Copyright ©2020 Mandy Murray

Cover photo – by Pandora De Pledge

Back cover photo – The Boudoir

Contents

Foreword – Double Dee, Strange Brew Radio

Prologue	1
Chapter one	3
Chapter two	11
Chapter three	24
Chapter four	55
Chapter five	65
Chapter six	76
Epilogue	80

Foreword

Life is a series of changes….. sometimes you know what direction you are heading and at other times you must go with what is in your heart. Mandy Murray tells her story of change, in her own words, something that many are afraid to bring to light. As a straight woman I have the same fears as Mandy and I was able to relate to her anxieties of being a woman. How do I dress, does it look flattering? How about my makeup…. too much? Will I be accepted? As a woman who suffers from the same anxieties that Mandy goes through during her transformation, I can relate to everything she says. This isn't just about putting on a dress, makeup and a wig, this is about life and what one must endure to be truly happy in one's own skin. It is also about being in a place where you are not judged by what or who you are but by the beautiful soul you are inside. A place where you feel welcomed and respected and above all loved. I believe everyone should read this story and ask themselves who they really are. You may be surprised at how much her story can help you write your own……

Double Dee, Strange Brew Radio

Prologue

9th September 2017

Hurricane Irma is heading to Florida and has Key West in its sights. It is due to make landfall on Saturday 9th September and all over that weekend a feeling of impending doom has settled over my house. I have remained in Key West before during a category one hurricane, but a category five like Irma is a completely different animal.
The TV is permanently on the weather channel, my laptop is monitoring the webcams around Key West and my radio is tuned (via the internet) to US1 Radio on Sugarloaf Key, who are doing a great job of keeping everyone informed. That is, until Irma arrived and the power failed and it all went dark.
However, I am not in Key West, I am in England, safe from the storm. I am not a Conch, not even American, so why am I so worried about what is happening 4000 miles away? Because my name is Mandy Murray, I am transgendered and Key West, where I have very many friends, is the place where I was reborn.

Like most TG people my story started a very long time ago……..

Chapter 1

People sometimes ask me why I became a crossdresser, I must confess that I am often tempted to say that I picked up a book in the library entitled 'Why Not Try Being A Transvestite' and thought I'd give it a go. It almost seems as though some people think that it is a temporary fad that odd people go through and that sooner or later they will grow out of.
However, being transgendered is something that you are born as, whether you realise it or not.
I learned at an early age that I preferred girl's clothes to boys but, due to our blinkered society that had been trained by religious ideals over the centuries to think of us as something to be reviled and persecuted, I believed that this was very wrong and that there must be something wrong with me.
Nevertheless it didn't prevent me from trying on my mother's clothes (where most of us male to female crossdressers start) which shows how strong the urge to be female is in a transgendered person.
I started with the usual of course, wearing my mum's knickers and bra and stuffing it with socks, but eventually graduated to trying on her dresses, skirts and shoes, while my feet were still small enough of course. I also tried putting on her makeup, badly of course.
This I did when my parents were out for the evening and it went on for many years, until an event occurred that changed things radically, my parents discovered what I had been doing.

Even after all these years it is still painful to remember this, which shows how much of a taboo crossdressing was, and still is, in our 'enlightened' world.

My parents of course had made the assumption that I must be gay, or homosexual as it was then still called, which at that time was not tolerated in England, which goes some way to explain their reaction, but didn't lessen the impact that it had on me. The next day, after many tears all around, I told my mother that I wasn't gay but I don't think that she fully believed me. Nonetheless she told me that no matter what *'I would always be her son'* and after more tears we embraced. This however was not the end of it, my father didn't want to talk to me when he arrived home from work that day and I was banished to the small bedroom that my sister usually occupied so as not to be a 'corrupting influence' on my younger brother. Of course it also meant that my brother was now sharing a bedroom with our older sister, but I guess my parents thought that this was the lesser of two evils.

Things settled down in the end of course but my parents always had their doubts about me which were only set aside when I got married some years later.

It did of course have a negative effect on my crossdressing activities as the items of clothing were very difficult to get my hands on but the feelings did not go away.

This story is probably very similar to many crossdressers' experiences, even now when, largely due to the internet, things are much easier for the community and people are (slowly) becoming more accepting. It is true to say that the gay community has done a remarkable job in the last forty years and gays and lesbians are now protected by law from discrimination (as are we) and are not only very visible in society but can now marry, and in the UK can now do this in church! What a turnaround from the institution that used to consider it against God's will 'to lie with another man'. Nonetheless the transgendered community is still very much in the dark ages compared to the gay community. This is probably mainly due to the fact that the majority of male crossdressers are heterosexual and are in relationships with women, who often don't know, so coming out to fight for the community as gays did is very difficult.

Of course, many trans people have fought for the cause and have helped the community enormously. When I first ventured out in public years later I was helped immensely by a certain lady who founded the TG friendly Way Out Club and the Tranny Guide in the UK. In fact it was her then partner who first did a makeover for me and escorted me to a tranny bar but more on that later.

What is it about wearing women's clothes that is so attractive to people like me. Well, initially, as with most CD's it was a big turn on. Nowadays it's a completely natural thing as I now identify as a woman and for me it has become the norm.

Transgendered people come in many variations, from the thrill seeker who wears his wife's knickers when she is out, to the full on transsexual who is either pre or post op and moving towards living as a woman full time. It is true that I started out at the transvestite stage wearing women's underwear just because I wanted to, but I moved on from that many years ago, as I developed into a crossdresser wearing women's clothes because that is what I saw myself as, a woman, albeit in the wrong body. In my youth I stayed pretty much in the first stages and when I got married I came out to my wife early on. I am ashamed to say that I didn't tell her before we married but there you are, we all have our failings. We worked it out and after a while I was able to wear some nice underwear in bed though she was never very comfortable with it. This situation carried on for many years even though my feelings of being feminine continued to grow. At that time the internet, as we now know it, didn't exist and it was very hard to discover things about being transgendered. Nowadays the web is full of clubs, advice, societies and shops, (both virtual and on the high street) where a T girl can learn all about dressing, makeup, hair and wigs and where to go when you have put it all together. Oh, if only I had had access to all of that when I was in my early twenties, how much fun I could have had. This is one of the reasons that I didn't make my first public appearance until I was much older, because I knew so little about that world.

Prior to this I had been living and working in London for a time and in this way I discovered such things as dressing services. My first experience of one of these was a big mistake. There is a chain of dressing services in the UK whose name I will not mention, suffice to say that they offer to 'transform' men who want to be female. Unfortunately, being made up (badly), given some rather worn clothes to wear and left in a room with a few magazines and soft porn videos for an hour or so wasn't what I was looking for. I moved on.

Not long after this I discovered a service run by a very nice trans lady called Caroline. Caroline offered a dressing service complete with an escorted trip out to a local bar, in this case the very well-known trans friendly Ted's Place in London's Earls Court. Just before this I had been experimenting a little more at home and, with the support of my wife, had ventured outside of our house wearing a dress, high heels, makeup (courtesy of my wife) a wig and a coat. It was definitely a scary experience but a necessary first step. Not wanting to shave and definitely being anti hairy legs, my wife had agreed to wax them for me. First time out this is a very painful experience but believe me, it does get easier (after a long time). So, wanting to venture further afield, with my wife's support, I booked a makeover with Caroline.

I travelled to London and made my way to the address that she had given me. She greeted me wearing full makeup and invited me in. She then proceeded to do a makeover for me that was light years apart from what I had experienced at 'the other place' and, after dressing in some rather nice clothes that my wife had lent me, we headed out to the bar. Ted's place was a nice little bar in a basement and we spent a couple of hours there chatting with other trans girls who frequented the place. After a while Caroline told me that she had to go to Soho to a night club called Madam Jojo's as she had some business to discuss with a colleague. She very kindly asked me if I would like to go with her to which I very eagerly said yes and offered to drive her there in my car.

Soho is internationally famous for its nightlife, strip clubs and late night bars and Madam Jojo's was a very famous burlesque night club which had a regular drag show. We parked my car on the street about a quarter of a mile away and walked to the club. Even though it was very busy I was quite cool about this as I was with Caroline, but when we arrived I was surprised to find that the place was full of regular guys and girls enjoying a night out. As far as I could tell we were the only trans girls in the place. I watched the show and drank a couple of cokes but around midnight I decided that I needed to head home as I had a two hour drive ahead. I thanked Caroline for a wonderful night and headed up the stairs to the street. Can you guess what happened next? I stepped out onto the street in the middle of Soho, late at night, wearing women's clothes, make up and a wig and my car was, what seemed at the time, miles away, and I was on my own! You have to remember that this was my very first experience of being out like this and the street was by no means quiet as there were many late night revellers out and about. As I very nervously started down the street towards my car a strange thing happened. Along the way I passed doorways of clubs and bars where bouncers stood guard. Every one of them called out to me as I passed asking if I was OK and wishing me good night. With my short dress and high heels I guess they must have thought that I was a working girl but I was so grateful to them for looking out for me. This really demonstrated to me how vulnerable a woman can feel in a situation such as this and it was a revelation. All men should be required to do this just once to understand what it is like for a woman on her own, maybe then they might decide to act a little bit more like gentlemen when seeing a woman on her own at night, maybe.

So, I had had my first public night out and in a place where it is totally impossible not to be noticed. Many more experiences were to follow which I will tell you about later in my story but for now, after a very long gestation period, Mandy had arrived!

Now, when I walk up Duval Street, the place where it all happens in Key West, with its many bars, restaurants, shops and tourists crowding the sidewalk, I sometimes think back to the days when I first nervously ventured out. But then I think about all of the experiences that I have had since then, in the UK and more lately in Key West. Then a big smile comes over my face and, in my mini skirt and high heels, I strut my stuff up to my favourite bar, La Te Da and feel like a million dollars.

Chapter 2

In these days of instant access to the world via the internet it's easy for trans women to make friends, search online stores, locate dressing services and find out about good trans friendly clubs. It has made it so much easier for a young trans person to get out into the big wide world and experience life to the full. However, when I first stepped out, even though the internet was up and running, most information came via books, guides and newsletters. At the time I was working in London in the music industry so it was easy for me to check out likely venues and find out about trans shops and makeover services. As mentioned earlier I had been introduced to the feminine world of epilation via leg waxing so I was also on the lookout for a suitable salon.

In the early 90's a lady by the name of Vicky Lee, who is famous in the trans world, was just launching something called the Tranny Guide. Initially this was a short black and white publication offering advice on all things that the aspiring trans girl should know. I got hold of a copy and found it to be of immense value. Vicky also started a club, The Way Out Club, which is now justly famous around the world. I owe this lady a huge debt, without her I doubt very much that I would have achieved all that I have since I first stepped out. In the early days the Way Out Club moved venues quite regularly, starting off in and around the West End of London before ending up in its current location in The City. Vicky's main problem was convincing owners of night clubs around town to give over one night a week to the TG community. Thank God that she persevered as, due to her, hundreds, if not thousands of people have enjoyed the great entertainment and social interaction in a safe venue over the years. I was able to visit the Way Out Club regularly in its various locations over the next fifteen years or so and this helped enormously with the development of Mandy.

In the early days I also discovered a dressing service in North London that came to be very important to me. It was called 'Girls Like Us' and I became a regular. The lady who ran it was a very talented makeup artist (I have been lucky enough to meet a few like her over the years) and she not only helped me to look great in makeup but also encouraged me to grow my hair long and style it in a feminine way. This was the first incarnation of Mandy. Though now I usually wear a wig which I really like, at the time it was great to be able to style my own hair. Though at this time I was gaining in confidence, on my first visit I had to park some distance away across a busy high street and after my makeover I had to ask her to escort me back to my car. It was early on a Friday evening and the streets were full of people on their way home from work, very nerve-racking!

'Girls Like Us' had a studio in a basement where they arranged photo shoots for their clients. This was an amazing experience as they really made you feel like a model. I booked a session and arrived ready for my makeover and photo shoot with a few different outfits. I still have the photos from this (colour prints, this was before digital photography) and I treasure them. It may sound a little conceited but in those photos I look fantastic. Sadly 'Girls Like Us' was forced to close a few years later so I had to find another makeover service. Of course I did and I have been lucky to work with some very talented people since, but I will always remember those wonderful early makeovers.

Buying new clothes was an experience. Things like false boobs and underwear, to flatten out the unsightly bulge between the legs, could be bought from specialist shops like Doreen's Fashions in East London. These places were very helpful and supportive of the TG community and really looked after us. I visited Doreen's where I bought my very first pair of silicon boobs. If you have ever seen any of these you will know that they feel incredibly realistic when worn under a bra. It often amazes male admirers when you let them touch you, over the top of clothes of course! Doreen's still exists today but rising rents on the high street where they had their store have forced them to close the shop and go completely online. They still have a great selection of things that every T girl needs and are still looking after our community after 60 years!

So, where to buy things like skirts, dresses, tops and tights? Well, the specialist shops have these as well of course, but if you want a bigger selection, as I did at the time, you need to go to the high street stores. Going into Marks and Spencer for the first time to buy a nice pair of knickers and some tights takes some courage, I can tell you. It's all available online now of course but not when I started out. Funny thing though, it turns out that their staff are trained to be very polite and, on the surface at least, not at all judgemental, so the only one who was embarrassed was me.

Now I find that there are lots of great stores online where I can buy great fashion clothes and stores like H&M, Gap and Next are fine if you want to try things on before you buy, best when made up though. Shoes come from stores like Long Tall Sally who cater for the lady with (ever so slightly) larger feet. Like most girls I can't have too many pairs of shoes and this tends to become somewhat of an addiction. My wardrobe is a bit over loaded with all of my female clothes these days still, a girl's gotta have a hobby!

I remember one occasion when I had been for another photo shoot at Girls Like Us and, having mentioned that I was going to the Way Out Club, the photographer, a real girl, asked if she could come with me. We had a great time at the club, talking with other T girls and spending lots of time on the dance floor. In the early hours my new friend suggested that we hit the streets in Soho as it was summer and the night was very warm. Game for anything I immediately agreed (I was staying in town anyway) and we headed out. Though it was some years ago I still remember that night clearly. I had on a little black dress and high heels and we walked through streets busy with other night owls coming out of clubs and hitting the all night coffee bars. We decided to get a coffee and whilst my friend sat at a table on the pavement I went inside to get the drinks. Whilst in the queue a lady came up to me and, out of the blue, told me that I looked great and said well done! She was congratulating me on having the courage to be myself in public. It was one of those rare moments when, venturing out into the 'real world', you discover that some people actually like and respect us trans women. This gave me a taste for going out to straight bars and clubs rather than being hidden away in safe tranny clubs and it led on eventually to the Mandy that struts her stuff on Duval Street amongst all of the tourists.

Compliments mean an awful lot to trans people. To have a regular person stop and say you look great is one of nicest things non trans people can do. We are all very nervous and aware that we are trying to look as real as we can and be accepted. Last year I was waiting for a taxi with two friends in Key West, standing outside a hotel on Eaton Street (a very busy road in rush hour) with a big queue of traffic with people making their way home. There were two women in a 4x4 and one of them wound the window down and said 'You look beautiful'. Thinking that she must have meant one of the ladies that I was with I pointed towards my companion but the woman said 'No, you!' That made me feel great for the whole night. If you are OK about trans people (as you are reading this story you probably are) and you meet one who has made the effort to look their best, just tell them that they look good, they will very much appreciate it. Some T girls reading this might say that it's all very well for me to say this, as I look OK but really, it isn't that difficult. There are plenty of people who will show you how to apply makeup and do your hair and, if you practice, practice and practice, you can achieve a good look for yourself. We can't all look like supermodels but there is no excuse to look like a man in drag just because you don't try your best. It does our community no good at all. I read an e mail recently where a trans club was promoting their next event. It said that now the nights were getting longer they expected more people to attend. This is very sad. If we do things properly girls we really shouldn't have to hide in the dark.

The years that followed saw me as a regular visitor to the Way Out Club, both solo and with some of the many friends that I made there. We had some great nights meeting up first and going to fashionable London restaurants amongst the 'normal' people (safety in numbers).

After Girls Like Us closed I found a lady who did makeovers from her house in North London and, after a few visits with her that went well, she agreed to come to my hotel to do my makeovers, so that I could go straight into town afterwards. By this time I had given up on trans friendly hotels like the famous Philbeach in Earls Court (a fine hotel but I wanted to go up market) and had started frequenting some of the top London hotels where I often stayed for business. As I often say, if you are paying the price that they charge they are not going to complain about what you wear. At this time Vicky decided to hold the Way Out Club's second birthday party at Stringfellows, owned by Peter of the same name. I went along to this as, not only was the venue quite famous, but I had been there a couple of times as my male self working in the music industry. It was quite amusing to me to be staying in the same hotels and visiting the same clubs as both a man and a woman, a little exciting too if I am honest.

I was still mostly paying for professional makeovers every time I went out, with occasional efforts of doing it myself. Applying makeup correctly is not really a problem once you have been taught how to do it. The problem is, unlike real women, whose mums teach them the mysteries from an early age, us trans females have to find out for ourselves and, even when once learned, don't do it every day. In many cases T girls only get the chance to go out dressed once a month or so and, as the well-known phrase goes, 'use it or lose it'. Without regular practice you are constantly having to re learn, which is why it is so much easier to go to a professional, providing you have the money.

It was around this time that I found the next professional makeup artist who had a major impact on my life as Mandy. Sadly she is no longer with us having passed away a few years ago, but many will know of her as she was a legend, Pandora De Pledge. Pandora was responsible for the second incarnation of Mandy and created for me a totally different look. Some of the photos of me during this time are on my Facebook page and they regularly receive wonderful compliments. Once I was even described as a supermodel, high praise indeed!

My hair was not quite as thick as it had been nor as long, so Pandora persuaded me to invest in a real hair wig. This, combined with her exceptional makeup skills, made me look quite stunning and I thoroughly revelled in going out to London's nightclubs looking fabulous. On one such night out I met two T girls from Sweden at the Way Out Club. They were over on a short vacation and we hit it off famously. I met up with them quite a few times after that on their subsequent visits and on one occasion, when all made up and meeting in our hotel rooms for a pre night out drink, I experienced something for the first time. Now, as I have said earlier, most crossdressers are heterosexual and I counted myself amongst them. Oddly though now, when out as my trans self, I still feel the same, but as I now completely identify as female, I am attracted to the opposite sex, i.e. men. I adore compliments from guys and love being treated as a lady. I have yet to take it all the way and may never do, but the feeling is there. I still love women but it's more about loving being one. I suppose in a way I must be bisexual but whatever I am I don't really care. The only important thing to me is to be my female self. Anything else that may or may not happen I leave to fate. When I was in that hotel room having our early cocktail one of the girls, Rebecca and I, felt an attraction towards each other and we kissed. It was obvious that we both enjoyed it immensely and, if it wasn't for her friend being in the room, things may well have gone on from there. However it didn't, but I will never forget that first T girl kiss. Was I attracted to her because she was a guy who looked like a woman, or because I was a lesbian, or because I was gay? It all gets so confusing when you swap genders. I don't really know but, as Katy Perry might have said, 'I kissed a T girl, and I liked it!" - Mandy mark 2 was moving up in the world!

As I have said before, in the early stages of coming out as a trans woman it is very difficult, even terrifying at times, to come out in public. Each time that you do make a successful trip out though it gets a little easier. In my early Mandy days in Key West I was holidaying with my wife who was being very supportive. On a couple of occasions she helped me with my makeup and even went out to the bars with me. Still nervous and not realising how friendly the town was I would stay back on the porch of the house we were renting and wait for the taxi before making a quick dash for it when it arrived. On one occasion I was hanging back waiting for a cab when a guy came by on a scooter (a popular form of transport in Key West). He saw me (almost) hiding in the bushes and stopped and asked "Ma'am, are you OK?" Well, being called Ma'am and asked if I was OK did wonders for my confidence I can tell you.

Key West doesn't have any tranny clubs, not that I have discovered anyway. There is a very good reason for this, it's because we are welcome in regular bars (with possibly one or two exceptions) because this wonderful island is so gay friendly. This is what makes it a paradise for us trans women. It does have a couple of drag bars though, Aqua and 801, which host drag shows every night. 801 is run by a very famous lady named Sushi who is occasionally seen on the stage herself. She also officiates at many of the events in town throughout the year, in particular New Year's Eve when she is lowered from the rooftop in an enormous high heeled shoe at the stroke of midnight, no really!

A word here about the Key West drag queens. They are an institution who do an enormous amount of work for local charities. Each year, based around events such as Valentine's Day, Fourth of July, Gay Pride, Mother's Day and of course the annual Fantasy Fest Parade, the drag queens hold events to raise money for good causes. In particular is the annual 'Drag Race' on Duval Street. Nothing to do with cars but a lot to do with high heels and a lot of laughs. These wonderful ladies raise thousands of dollars each year for local charities and are very much a part of the Key West community. They are to be applauded.

One night I was in the audience at 801 watching Sushi on stage doing her act. She saw me in the audience and pulled me up onto the stage. After the usual (inevitable) jokes she got serious and told the audience that the girls in the show did this for a job, but people like me did it for real and that it took a great deal of courage to do so.

The whole room applauded and one guy in the audience insisted on giving me a tip in the traditional way that they do it there, a dollar bill tucked into my undies.

This, I can tell you, did wonders for my budding confidence. Thanks Sushi!

One day I was walking along Margaret Street in Old Town Key West where I was renting an apartment. As I approached the junction with Fleming Street I saw an unusual looking man standing on the sidewalk. He was dressed all in black, jeans, shirt and waistcoat and had jet black hair with a matching beard. Now, this is not the usual type of dress that one expects to see in a tropical island where shorts and brightly coloured tops are the norm. As I got nearer he saw me and walked towards me, not knowing what to expect I stopped and a little nervously, said hello. He then gave me a wrist band with the words 'One Human Family' written on it. At once I knew (as will any resident of KW reading this who will have instantly recognised my description of him) that this was none other than JT Thompson, the (justly famous) man who invented the slogan 'One Human Family' – 'Unity, Equality, Diversity'. In 2000 this was adopted as the official philosophy of Key West and later on for the whole of the Florida Keys. It certainly sums up the wonderful accepting qualities of everyone who lives and works in the Conch Republic.

JT is regularly seen around town and officiating at some of the many fund raising events that happen on the island. His motto and the wrist bands and stickers that he produces, have been sent all over the world and thousands of people now subscribe to his wonderful philosophy. Perhaps one day the 'One Human Family' slogan will be the motto of the whole world. I hope so and proudly wear my wrist band all of the time.

Chapter 3

Scandal! No, I haven't been exposed in the Sunday papers, it's a film about a very famous period in British History. In the 1960's, when London was swinging and the centre of the music and fashion industries, there was a girl called Christine Keeler. Christine was a model who was fated to bring about the downfall of a senior minister and discredit the British Government.

There is much information online about the Profumo Affair as it came to be called, suffice to say that Christine had an affair with John Profumo, the then minister for war, whilst at the same time also having a relationship with a Russian naval attaché and intelligence officer. When you remember that this was at the height of the cold war this wasn't such a good idea. Anyway, the press got hold of this and all hell broke loose. Christine, and her best friend Mandy Rice-Davies, suddenly became very famous and whilst all of this was going on Christine posed for what is now a very well-known photograph, ostensibly for a movie which was never released in the UK. This photo, which has Christine appearing to pose nude, whilst sitting in a chair based on a design by Arne Jacobsen, was shot in black and white and became almost as famous as her affair and epitomised the rather cool feel of the time.

I became fascinated with this story and found the photo to be very erotic so I decided that I needed to re-create it. I contacted the lady who was now doing my makeovers, Jodie Lynn at The Boudoir, another very famous dressing service and explained my idea. Jodie also has a photo studio so I provisionally booked a makeover and photo session and set out to find the famous chair. Googling Arne Jacobsen gave me a lot of info about the designer and then, courtesy of the internet, I tracked down a company that had similar chairs for hire. I managed to persuade them to give me a fair rate for the hire and delivery of just one chair (they normally hire out lots of these for conferences and such) and deliver it to Jodie's studio.

When the big day came I arrived with my things (not wanting to waste a great makeover I was going out to a club afterwards) including a fur coat (imitation) that I liked to wear in the winter. Jodie's father was the photographer and I have to say that he did a fantastic job. I was naked apart from a small thong for decencies sake, and I have a great collection of black and white photos to treasure. The best one of these got posted on Facebook and various other social networking sites and attracted a lot of interest and favourable comments. I don't know if Christine Keeler ever saw it but it was a brilliant recreation of the famous shot from the 60's. When we had enough photos of me in the chair he took some of me wearing the fur coat (and nothing else, apart from the thong of course) so I had some more great photos to use as well. All in all a great success, thanks to Jodie and her dad.

P.S. Mandy Rice-Davies was the inspiration for my name, we all have our heroes, or heroines.

Photographs are very important to T girls, even more so than regular people I would suggest. If you have spent money for a professional makeover and can only be your real self occasionally, then you want to have something to remember it by. Most of the makeover professionals that I have met will also arrange photo shoots like The Boudoir. Even those who don't have photo studios will often offer to take a selection of photos at the end of the makeover. And in these days of digital photography there is always the ever popular 'selfie'.

Fortunately, not only is it easier to shoot lots of photos of that special occasion, but it is far easier to store all of those great shots on your computer or smart phone. I for one have literally hundreds of photos from nights out in the UK and more latterly from Key West. Many of these are available to view on my Facebook page.

As I touched on earlier, nowadays I prefer to do my own makeovers before going out. Over the years I have managed this with varying degrees of success but now I am feeling quite confident in this. Like I said it needs constant practice to do it well and now that I spend a couple of months in Key West each year living full time as Mandy I get to do it every day. It wouldn't be practical to have it done every day by a professional, and it would cost too much as well, so I had to learn to do it properly myself. I do get lots of compliments on my looks when I am out and about so I guess I can't be all that bad.

I did use the services of a very talented lady called Flower, who worked at Headlines Beauty Parlour in Key West, a few times in my early days there. On one such occasion I had called for a cab to take me back to my rental house and, when it picked me up from Headlines the cab driver, who was a lady, asked me if I had been to the salon the have my hair done! Wow, not only a compliment on my hair style but she didn't seem to notice that I was trans, or if she did she was too polite to mention it. That's Key West for you.

As well as practicing doing my own makeup I have recently come across a very wonderful lady called Michelle who sells a well-known line of cosmetics from her home in the UK. Not only has she offered me invaluable advice on what to buy and helped me replace some of my cheaper makeup items with better quality ones, she also very kindly agreed to give me a one on one makeup tutorial at home. This was extremely useful and I made lots of notes so that I didn't forget what she taught me.

In the past I have used theatrical makeup to cover the darker areas on my face that are still there even after a very close shave. It's a problem all of us T girls have unless we go in for epilation or laser treatment on our faces. I have it in mind to try it one day, maybe. The problem with the thick pan stick cover-up is that it is sticky, even after applying finishing powder. Michelle was able to suggest a better type of foundation that not only does the job but is completely dry after application so I don't get that irritating feeling of stray hairs from my wig sticking to my cheeks. The best thing however that Michelle put me on to are fibre lashes. I have always had a problem applying false eyelashes and have experienced them peeling off when I'm in a bar trying to look sexy over a glass of wine, not good. I have to tell you that these fibre lashes are the perfect answer. They are very easy to apply with the brush and really make your eyelashes two or three times as long. You can bat your eyelids at the hunk across the room with complete impunity. Well, from the prospect of peeling lashes that is, can't say what the guy might do though.

The latest thing that I have heard about is a lip plumper. You apply this like a lipstick and it makes you look like you have had collagen implants. I have just ordered one of these from Michelle and can't wait to try it.

Two other ladies here in England have been of tremendous help to me in my journey to be my true self. First I must mention Nicky who has been my hairdresser for many years and has also become my confident and good friend of Mandy. She has been the source of good advice on my appearance, has helped me to purchase suitable wigs (and washes and styles them for me) and has also accompanied me to bars and restaurants in my local area here in Oxfordshire.

Secondly is the lovely Donna. Donna is a beauty therapist and it is to her that I go to when I want my legs waxed, eyebrows waxed and eyelashes tinted, pedicures done (with painted toenails) and manicures. Donna introduced me to a fantastic type of manicure called gelish. When applied this creates a hard polish on the nails that will only come off with an acetone remover. I can have a clear gelish applied, or if I'm feeling daring can have it as a French polish that I wear even when not made up. I can then apply a normal nail polish in a bright colour over the top which can be taken off with regular remover leaving the clear gelish unharmed underneath, wonderful! I go to Donna for a full work over just before I set out for Key West so that I look my best. She is a treasure.

All three of these wonderful ladies not only help me with my appearance but are very supportive of me, once again proving that some people do like and respect us trans women, to you three ladies go my heartfelt thanks.

I have got the process of applying makeup and styling my hair down to around forty five minutes, which is great if I want to go shopping in Key West in the day, then come back to my rental, take it all off, shave and reapply it to hit the bars in the evening. There are plenty of shops on Duval Street like CVS where you can go to top up supplies, but if you want more specialist stuff then I can recommend Leather Master of Appelrouth Lane in Key West. It does have a rather interesting stock of leather apparel, plus great costumes for Fantasy Fest, but it also has a big range of specialist makeup items as well. I am told that this is where most of the drag queens go for their more theatrical makeup, and it carries lots of items that you won't get in the local Walgreens, and the guys in the store are really nice too and can offer advice if asked.

Let me tell you about my favourite bar in Key West, no in the whole world. It is called La Te Da and it is short for La Terraza Di Marti. It was named after a Cuban revolutionary from the nineteenth century, Jose Marti, who gave a famous speech from the balcony (La Terraza) when it was the private home of a Cuban cigar manufacturer.

In more recent times it has become a famous hotel / restaurant / cocktail bar that holds regular cabarets and is situated at the nicer end of Duval Street. I first encountered La Te Da during the run up to a hurricane around ten years ago. I was renting a house at the time and Hurricane Ike, which had at one stage been a category 4 but had reduced to a category 2, was heading for the Florida Keys. Earlier in my stay that year I had been in a hotel for a few days and had had to evacuate up to Miami when Hurricane Faye was heading in. In the end Faye downgraded and wasn't a problem but I had missed a couple of days in KW because of the evacuation order. When Ike appeared I was staying in the rented house with my wife and once again the state government issued a mandatory evacuation order for visitors but not for residents. Being reluctant to trek up to Miami again I called the rental agency and guess what? They told me that as I was renting a house I counted as a resident and didn't need to go. They also told me that they would fit hurricane shutters to the house and that we would probably be OK if we stayed. So, we stayed.

The day before Ike was due to arrive we walked down to the south end of Duval. The sun was shining, the sea was blue and the temperature was in the 80's. However, it was very quiet as the tourists had gone and most of the shops, bars and restaurants were boarded up, some with handwritten signs saying 'Take a hike Ike' (love their sense of humour). We walked along Duval and then heard music coming from a bar, we looked in the open door to see lots of people sitting around the bar drinking. At first we thought it was a private party but we ventured up to the door and looked inside. One of the people at the bar saw us and called out to us to come in. When we entered we asked if it was a private party and he said (you've guessed it) "No, it's a hurricane party!"

Now, I had heard of these before but had never encountered one (not so many hurricanes in the UK) but the idea is, that if a hurricane is coming which may cause damage and destroy life's important things like booze, then you might as well drink it all while you can. I don't think this is unique to Key West by any means and is common in the Caribbean, but it sure as hell sums up the spirit of the Conch Republic!

We had a very nice time at the hurricane party and returned to our rental to wait out the storm. In the end by the time it reached KW it had lost some of its power and was downgraded to a tropical storm with winds similar to what they get in the Scottish Hebrides. So it was the right thing not to evacuate.

Having 'discovered' La Te Da it became a very popular haunt of ours over the next few years. As I think I have mentioned before, a few times anyway... it is my absolute fave place in the world. Part of the reason for this is because, not only is it so very welcoming to all, as well as me as Mandy, but I have made lots of friends there. Next I will tell you about some of the people I have met at my favourite bar.

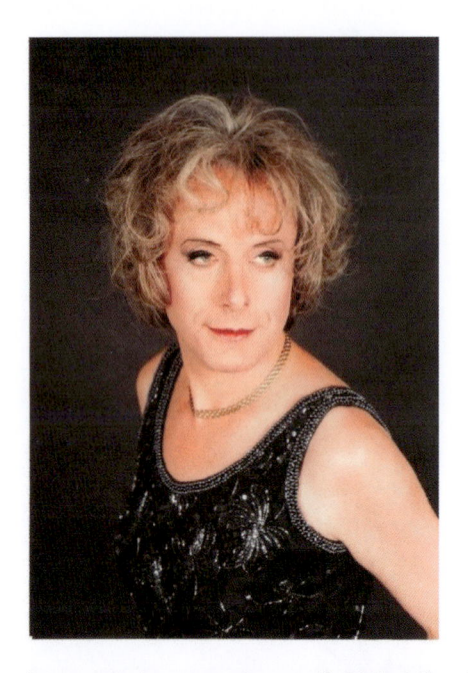

Mandy mark 1 – courtesy of Girls Like Us

Mandy mark 2 – courtesy of the sadly missed Pandora De Pledge

My friend Rebecca - I kissed a T girl and I liked it!

A wild birthday night at '801' – with one of the wonderful Key West drag queens

The famous Christine Keeler photo from the 1960's

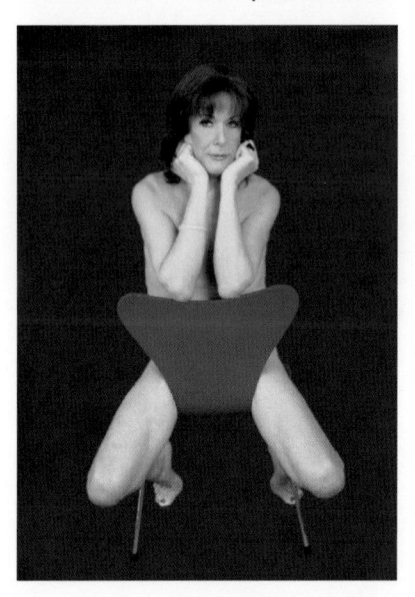

….. and my version of it

Good photos are important to T girls, but there is always the reliable 'selfie'

La Te Da on Duval Street – my favourite place in the world

At the outside bar at La Te Da – with the fabulous Tonto

With Jacqui, Sally, Sue and Marsha – 'we are family'

On Sue's scooter – wearing a white mini skirt, totally impractical!

With Sharon and Nina (Angel) two of my very best friends

At Hard Rock Café on Duval

The dancing 'queen' at La Te Da (I'm the one with her arms in the air)

'Baby Spectrelle' AKA Allison Mayer, performing with Dave Bootle at La Te Da

The Fabulous Spectrelles at The Bull on Duval……

…..and with their latest band member

Just four working girls taking a break

An older but favourite photo of mine - courtesy of Pandora De Pledge

Chatting with one of the KWPD at The Bull – this officer is a real star, I have seen him on stage at Aqua Idol many times helping to raise money for AIDS relief

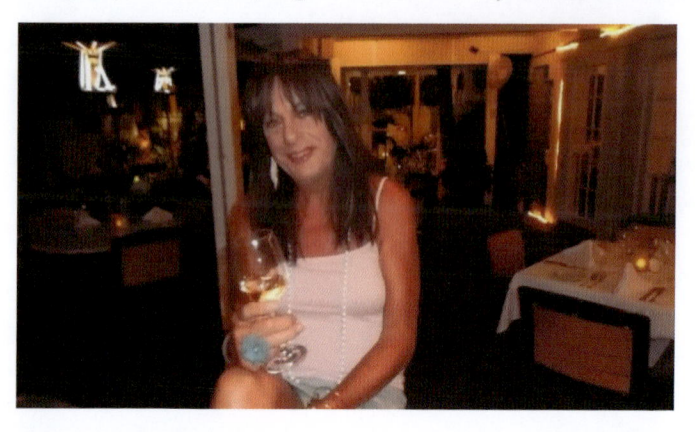

At one of my fave restaurants – Michaels in Key West

shorts or mini skirt? – the mini won!

Key West residents on stage for 'Aqua Idol

The very lovely and talented Traci

Mandy at the little black dress cocktail party

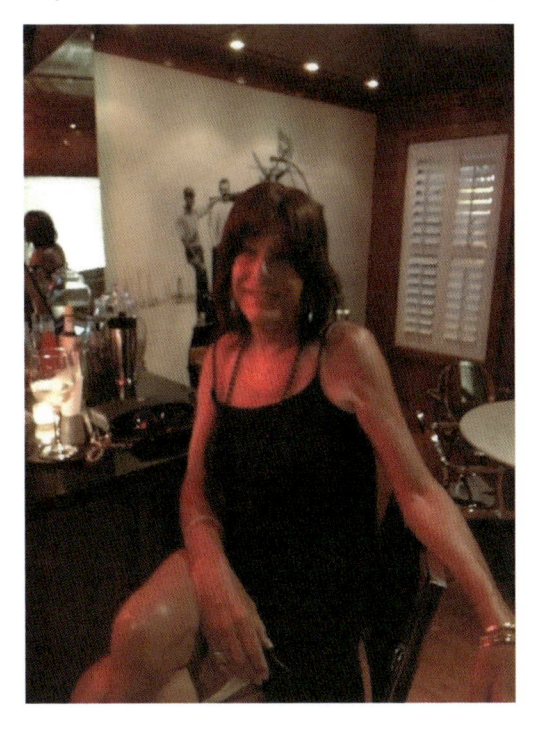

And after, at the very stylish Saints Hotel

with Mindy – a very dear friend

me and the 'Barbee' enjoying 'Bootle Bombs' on the local's parade

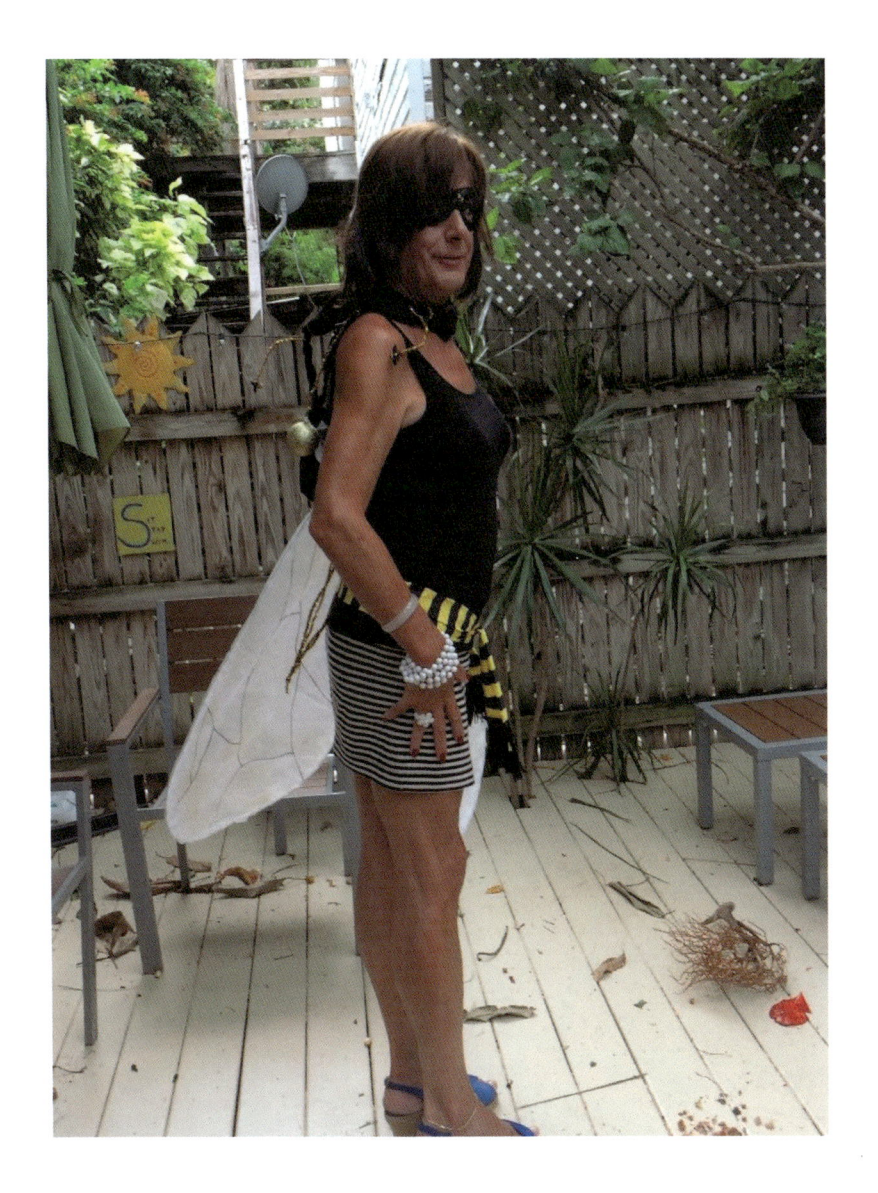

me as a 'new-bee'

Plenty of 'rest stations' en-route, with a choice of cocktails – red, or blue!

The start of the local's parade

the 'four bees'

My 'farewell' party at Mangoes in 2019

With 'Alan Alan Alan' (my guardian) at Mangoes

I had the honour to help carry the rainbow flag in the Pride Parade 2019

With Carter and EJ at the Island House pride party

and EJ's lovely wife Seann

Sister Louis Gabriel's Grotto

"As long as the Grotto stands, Key West will never experience the full brunt of a hurricane."

Chapter 4

In the last part of my story I left you standing at the bar at La Te Da. Sorry about that, but I bet someone came up to you to chat and offered to buy you a drink. Yes? Thought so, it's just that sort of place.

Let me tell you about some of the wonderful friends I have met standing at that very same bar (from both sides) where you are now.

I have made great friends amongst the staff, particularly Tonto, Casey, Michael, Claire and Mindy, not forgetting the current owner, Christopher. On one of my early visits to La Te Da as Mandy, the lovely Casey was working on the inside bar, where they have cabaret. I walked up to the bar, said hello and ordered a drink. Casey, who only knew me at that time in male mode, acknowledged me and then did a double take. Recognising the voice but not the face said "Steve, is that you?" I smiled and said yes to which she replied "You look beautiful", for that, I offered to buy her a drink!

I have also made lots of friends there amongst the customers, both residents of Key West and visitors. I don't know what it is about us but most people seem to be fascinated by T girls and want to chat, particularly the ladies (real ones that is). This usually happens at the bar, which of course results in lots of free drinks! On a couple of visits I have been there during 'women's week' which is a week-long celebration for, well, women. I have been literally mobbed by girls in the drag club 801 during women's week. The girls come down to Key West from all over the USA to celebrate it and quite often go crazy. Having a tranny in their midst is another wild thing that they accept when in Key West and in my experience they love it.

On one occasion during women's week I met four ladies there, two who lived in Miami and two who lived in Texas. They were on vacation together and usually went every year at the same time. We became great friends and spent a lot of time together both that year and also the following one. I'll never forget riding on the back of Sue's scooter in a white mini skirt after dinner, heading for La Te Da and then sitting at the outside bar singing 'We are family, I've got all my sisters with me' Thanks Sue, Marsha, Jacquie and Sally, it was great fun.

Another time I was sitting at the bar in Mandy mode when two ladies from West Palm Beach walked in. Quite quickly we got chatting (of course) and got on famously. These ladies were Sharon and Nina. For some reason I never got

Nina's name right at first so I nicknamed her Angel. The three of us spent lots of time on the dance floor dancing to The Fabulous Spectrelles (more on them later) including getting a photo with them on stage, plus spending a fair bit of time at the bar. By the end of the night we had become best pals and promised to keep in touch. The next evening I was back at La Te Da but for some reason I was in male mode. After a while in came Nina and Sharon who of course didn't recognise me as I was not dressed as Mandy. Realising this I said 'hello Angel' to Nina. She couldn't work out who I was at first as no one else called her by that name, but then the penny dropped and both Nina and Sharon were delighted to meet me in my alter ego. To quote Humphrey Bogart, this was the start of a beautiful friendship and these wonderful ladies have made the trip down from West Palm Beach every year since, just to meet up with me. On one occasion they were getting packed ready to drive down when their families asked them what they were doing. They said that they were going to Key West for a few days. Their families said that a hurricane was predicted to hit the Keys and that they must be crazy. Nina and Sharon said that they were going to Key West to meet their UK friend Mandy and that was that! Nina and Sharon arrived but the hurricane didn't, so all was well.

One night, sitting in The Little Jazz Room on Duval, Nina told me that she was a professional jazz saxophonist who played at the Newport Jazz Festival in New York in the 1960's. Wow! The people that you meet in Key West! Later that same night we went to The Bull on Duval (I told you that it all happens on that street) and went up to the top floor, known as The Garden Of Eden. The clue is in the name. This is a rooftop bar and dance floor that accepts full (discretionary) nudity. Now, neither Sharon, Nina nor I, took our clothes off but plenty of others did. We were dancing to some very loud house music when a rather happy young lady came up to me (not wearing anything) and asked me to take my top off. I pointed out that if I did, my false boobs would fall on the floor which wouldn't look very good. She had a good laugh at that and moved on. So did I...

Nina and Sharon are two of my very dearest friends and we have shared some wonderful times together. I will always love them.

As mentioned, lots of real girls seem very interested in us T girls and I get loads of invitations to dance when in the various bars in Key West. Sometimes these ladies literally drag me onto the dance floor and won't let me go afterwards but that's OK because (did I tell you?) I LOVE dancing.

Now, there is a guy called Dave Bootle, YES! Dave is a professional entertainer who plays piano and sings, mostly well-known cover songs but with a few of his own thrown in. Dave is without doubt far and away the best entertainer of this type that I have ever come across. He plays regularly at La Te Da as well as other places around town. He also plays at private parties and occasionally goes off to places like Bermuda to do a residency at a club there. Why is he so good? Because he has a great voice, really involves his audience, and plays the songs we all know and love. He has an enormous repertoire and is rarely caught out when people request songs. So, for someone who loves dancing (me) attending a Bootle show is absolutely the best night out!

I can literally spend the whole evening dancing to Dave (which plays havoc with the drinking) and one song in particular, always gets me on my feet, no matter where I hear it. It's a well-known Abba song which I am sure you are familiar with and whenever Dave plays it when I am in the room he says 'this is for Mandy, the dancing queen!' I rather suspect that there is a play on words here and 'queen' doesn't really relate to the girl in the song….

One night I was enjoying Dave's show (at La Te Da of course) and spending most of my time on the dancefloor, when I took a break to go to the ladies room. Yes that's right, ladies room. This isn't North Carolina! When I came back to the bar one of my friends, a local named Carter, handed me a cocktail as I walked in the door. Thanking him I looked around and realised that the 30 or so people in the room were all holding cocktails and standing up. Carter, and Dave Bootle, then offered a toast 'To Mandy' which everyone in the room echoed. How's that for being accepted! I was completely knocked out.

Dave asked me on one occasion why he never sees me these days in male mode. Not wishing to go into long explanations about how I see myself I simply asked him who he preferred. After a moment's thought he said Mandy. So there you are!

Earlier on I mentioned The Fabulous Spectrelles. These are a threesome girl group who regularly perform in various bars in Key West wearing beehive hairdos and sixties style clothes. They perform all the classic girl group songs of the era like 'It's My Party' 'Be My Baby' 'Mama Said' 'My Boyfriend's Back' 'Leader Of The Pack' and loads more and they are simply 'fabulous'. These girls pack the bars wherever they perform and I have seen people lining up on the sidewalk when the bars are full just to see them. I first met them three years ago and have memories of fantastic nights dancing to the great music. The Fabulous Spectrelles is owned and run by the lead singer Baby Spectrelle, otherwise known as Allison Mayer and I count her as another of my good Key West friends. She also performs solo as herself and has a fantastic voice. One night we met up for dinner at Michaels, a great Key West restaurant and after we walked over to La Te Da as Dave Bootle was playing. During the evening I manged to persuade Allison to perform a couple of songs with Dave and together they went down a storm.

A few years ago I decided to visit a friend of mine who lives in Tennessee before heading down to Key West. After a very pleasant few days in the home of the blues, I decided to drive to KW rather than fly. In that way I would get to see far more of the countryside than I would in a passenger jet. I expected it to take two or three days and booked my first night's hotel in Destin on the Florida Panhandle. I crossed over into Mississippi and spent the day driving south, surprised to find that it was quite hilly and wooded countryside. After an eight hour drive I arrived at my hotel in the early evening. Next day I decided to travel along the coast road as I had been told that the scenery was quite stunning. It was well worth it, the 'sugar sand' all along the coast was a powdery white and the sea a striking emerald blue. It's not called the emerald coast for nothing. Out of the panhandle I picked up the main highway south and after another eight hour drive I stayed at The Hilton on the beach in Clearwater. The next part of my journey took me through the Everglades and onto US1 towards the Florida Keys and Key West.

This is one of the most beautiful drives in the world as it links the chain of islands called keys, via forty two bridges and on both sides is the sea, the gulf on one side and the ocean on the other. The views are magnificent, with the colours of the shallow water in greens, blues and turquoises.
As I drove over the seven mile bridge, which links the upper Keys with the lower Keys, I was listening to the song 'Brothers In Arms' by Dire Straits. On my right to the west the last of the sun was setting into a purple sea and on my left in the east the moon was rising from the ocean. The line in the song 'Now the sun's gone to hell and the moon's riding high' had never seemed more appropriate and more beautiful.

I arrived in Key West in the late evening and, finding the place that I had rented, I got the key from the lock box and carried my things up to the second floor apartment. It had been a long journey and I wanted to sit on the balcony for a while. There was a sign in the apartment asking that visitors make sure the door to the balcony is shut when going outside because of the air conditioning. I dropped everything inside and, shutting the door behind me, I went onto the balcony. You may have guessed what's coming next but it took me completely by surprise. The balcony door was self-locking and I was shut outside, fifteen feet up in the air, with my keys, phone and everything else inside! All I had on was a short miniskirt and a skimpy top, (it was hot after all).

What to do? The balcony was mostly screened by a pair of very large palm trees so no one could see me. I didn't fancy climbing down them as they looked very prickly and even if I did, I couldn't get back into the apartment and I would be on the streets of Key West without money, phone or ID. In other words a (tranny) vagrant. Gives a new meaning to TV....

I tried calling down to people to ask for help, but with the noise from Duval Street a block away, most people didn't hear me and those that did were drunk and weren't interested in a strange voice seemingly coming from nowhere. Maybe they thought it was one of the Key West ghosts that are quite common there, or so I am told.

By now it was getting late, although the parties were still in full swing on Duval Street and I was getting quite worried. At last I managed to attract the attention of two ladies below me on the sidewalk. They looked up and saw me through the palm leaves and I told them about my predicament. They said don't you worry honey, we'll go find a cop, and off they went. A half hour passed and just as I was starting to worry again a cop car pulled up and one of Key West's finest got out. Having met some of these on occasions since, I have to tell you that they really are great guys and girls. They join in the many celebrations throughout the year and, off duty, many of them get heavily involved in charity events. The motto on their patrol cars reads 'protecting paradise' and that's just what they do.

This cop must have thought it a little unusual to see a scantily dressed trans woman locked out on her balcony but he didn't comment. After I explained to him what had happened he tossed up a rock for me to break the glass in the door but told me that when I had 'broken in' I had to go downstairs with my passport and rental proof. After all I might well have been a tranny burglar! All was well in the end though it did cost me for a replacement pane of glass the next day. As a post script, a few days later I had fallen asleep on the sofa after getting in late (something to do with alcohol) when I was awoken by someone calling for help from the rear of the apartment block. It turns out that I wasn't the only visitor who got locked out on the balcony!

Chapter 5

Not all of my life as Mandy has been positive though. Existing relationships can and do have a major impact. I have mentioned that my wife has been supportive of me in the past and that is true but times change. Though she has no objection to me wearing my clothes around the house she now objects to me doing my makeup when she is around. She has also stopped vacationing with me as she doesn't want to spend her time with Mandy. We have come to an agreement on all this which works for us so far. Though she has accompanied me as my true self in the past she doesn't want to do that anymore so this has led to us pretty much leading separate lives for a large part of our time.

Another problem is my daughter. I don't mean that she is a problem as I love her dearly, but she is living at home currently and though she knows about me she really doesn't want to see me being in any way feminine. So, at home in the UK, apart from odd nights out, I pretty much have to pretend to be someone that I am not. Of course, my daughter wants to see me as the dad that I have always been, at least on the surface and I fully understand that, but where does it leave me? As mentioned earlier, a person doesn't choose to become transgender, whether you choose to act on the feelings or not, if you are born transgender you will always be transgender. There are no cures for this, much as many sections of society would like there to be. I won't even get into the things that were done to TG people in the not so distant past, suffice to say that electric shock treatment and insane asylums were the accepted cures in times gone by.

Even if there was a cure, how many of us would take it? The very word 'cure' implies that there is some disorder that one needs curing from. What is 'normal' very much depends on how the majority of a society view things. I certainly don't see myself as being in any way ill, so why would I need a cure? I am proud of who I am and grateful to the people of that tiny island at the end of US1 for treating me as just a normal person. If I was offered a magic pill, to make my female side go away, I would very quickly throw it in the trash.

As for old friends of mine in the UK who do not know me as Mandy I have this to say: one of the girls that I met in Key West regularly posts thoughts on Facebook and one she posted a couple of years ago has stayed with me. *'If you are being true to yourself and it's not good enough for the people around you, then change the people around you.'* That works for me!

It hasn't always been so. I have read that other civilisations (non Judeo Christian religions) have, in the past, honoured and respected us of the in-between sex. After all we do have experience of looking at it from both sides, so to speak. Maybe one day it will be that way again, I do hope so. There does seem to be a lot more sympathetic attention from the media these days, certainly in the UK anyway. I am reading almost daily about young people going for gender reassignment surgery, schools treating kids, who identify as the opposite sex to how they were born, in a fair and supportive manner. Parents seem to be more understanding these days and come out publically in support of their TG children and documentaries about transgender issues are becoming more common place on television. All of this is happening in an open and honest way with none of the ridiculing undertones that were so obvious in the past. Even Doctor Who, the long running BBC Television character, has recently had a sex change! Maybe things are really changing and kids who are born as the wrong sex in the future will be able to rectify it without all the obstacles that were placed in front of us just a few years ago.

I love my family dearly but I am who I am and I have no desire to change. When I am in Key West, as mentioned before, I live full time as myself and am extremely happy. This is because I feel whole, the way I was meant to be and am utterly content. The longer that I spend there each year the happier I am. Coming back to the UK is always a bitter time as I feel that the major part of me is missing and this upsets me greatly. Each year that I return it gets harder and harder and when I drive up US1 on my way to Miami airport for a flight to London, I keep repeating to myself over and over, you're going the wrong way girl!

I have to come back for two reasons, one is my family and the other are the US immigration laws. The maximum time that I can stay in the States is six months and though I haven't been able to do this yet I intend to as soon as possible. There is another problem related to this. Unlike the Florida mainland, property in the Keys, particularly in Key West, is horrendously expensive. A simple one bedroom apartment can set you back half a million dollars, and for this reason rentals are also astronomically high. Nonetheless I am totally convinced that it is my true home and am determined to live there one day.

Maybe I am coming to a watershed in my life and something will have to give. I know that my true self is feminine and this will not be denied. I am Mandy and will forever be so, come what may.

Lately, I have been feeling that something special awaits Mandy in Key West. I don't know what it is, whether it is something that I will do for the good of others or something (good I hope) that will happen to me, but I believe that my destiny awaits me in the Conch Republic, so let's return to that paradise island in the turquoise blue sea and order another margarita, after all, it is 5 O'clock somewhere!

Last year I treated myself to a very brief pair of denim shorts. I reckon I have the legs and the ass for these so why not. I decided to try them out one morning when I was going to Faustos, the local supermarket, for a few provisions. Having put my face on and sorted my hair off I went. Got a few appreciative looks from a couple of guys in the store and took my things up to the cash desk. The lady cashier looked at me and said "you look great in those shorts honey, you sure have the legs for them". So, later that day I posted two pictures on Facebook, one of me wearing the shorts and one wearing a mini skirt and asked people which they preferred. The shorts got a couple of votes but the mini skirt won hands down. Should have guessed really ….

I have mentioned Fantasy Fest a couple of times. I guess most people know all about this Key West version of Mardi Gras but having experienced this recently I would like to tell you about my experiences. It's true that the main parade which happens on the last Saturday in October is a fantastic spectacle that takes place on Duval Street when Key West really lets its hair down, yes, more so than normal! However, the whole event runs for a week and lots of things happen on the run up to the main parade. All of this is about collecting money for charity (as well as partaking of your favourite beverage, in huge amounts) and one of the big things that happens is the annual Fantasy Fest King and Queen contest. This actually starts much earlier towards the end of summer, when people who wish to compete for the title first put their names forward. Once the candidates are announced, usually two for King and two for Queen, events are held around KW to raise money for AIDS charities, including a very funny 'karaoke pop idol' event at Club Aqua on Duval. 'Aqua Idol' is great entertainment and many residents of Key West take part, with each week taking on a different theme. If you are ever in Key West in the fall, get along to one of these that happen on Tuesday nights from early September during the run up to the main event at the end of October, it's well worth it.

I met a lovely lady called Traci who was once a member of the Fabulous Spectrelles. She is an extremely kind person and whenever I have been in town we have met up for a drink and a chat. We did this one night in Aqua for the Idol performance and we talked and talked and talked for ages. Traci has an amazing voice and was also performing in the show. Afterwards we chatted for hours about all sorts of things, just two girls enjoying each other's company. Traci has now moved to Las Vegas so I don't know if I will see her again, I hope so.

Another event that takes place on behalf of one of the candidates for queen is a 'little black dress cocktail party' at least it has for the last two years and I attended both of those. The first time it was a bit nerve wracking. My good friend Mindy persuaded me to go and assured me all would be fine. I had brought a black mini skirt on vacation with me and also had a black strappy top so I put the two together and hey presto! I had a little black dress. I found the address where this was due to take place and took a cab to the condo overlooking the beach. This was a block of private apartments and when I arrived it was very quiet with no one about. I was on my own and very nervously took the elevator up to the right floor. Not knowing the people who lived there I was totally unaware of how I would be received and what they would think about an English tranny turning up on their doorstep. Trusting to Mindy that everything would be alright I pushed the bell and was welcomed in by the owner of the apartment, a lovely lady who made me feel very welcome, as did all of the other people who were there. I had a fabulous evening chatting to all of the guests and meeting the candidate for queen and did my bit to raise money on the night for the charity. The next year I again went to a little black dress party, this time in a gorgeous house near the beach owned by a local doctor. Not at all nervous this time I had another great night, drinking champagne, meeting lots of lovely ladies and getting my photo in the local paper.

Also last year I attended the crowning of the victorious King and Queen at the Casa Marina Hotel along with my friends from West Palm Beach, Nina and Sharon. The winners are the ones that collect the most money from their various events and, after the crowning, officiate at all charity events throughout the coming year. Last year $380,000 was raised for AIDS relief, how fantastic is that! And the guy who became King was none other than Christopher, the owner of La Te Da!

As I was going to be there for the whole of Fantasy Fest I really wanted to take part in the main parade on the Saturday instead of watching it from the sidewalk. I had visions of skimpy bikinis and big feather headdresses. Enquiring as to how I could go about joining a float I was told that I could but I had to pay $150. Deciding that this was too much I politely declined but my good friend Mindy (I mentioned her before) came to my rescue.

Mindy is one of my best friends in Key West and a wonderful person. I first met her at La Te Da a few years ago and we have been good friends ever since. We get together often for drinks and sometimes get out on the water to enjoy the sea, sun and sand (the waters around Key West are beautiful and if you can get out on a boat there are some wonderful places to go, and you'll almost certainly see dolphins too). Anyway, Mindy told me about the 'locals' parade' which takes place on the Friday, the day before the main parade. This is a walking parade which the locals take part in dressed in wonderful costumes and parade along the streets of the town, stopping at 'drink stations' along the way. Some of these are provided by the hundreds of spectators, many of whom have cool boxes filled with various types of cocktails.

Mindy was taking part in the parade with two friends, Sheila and Alesha and they invited me to join them. They were to be dressed as bees, to highlight the plight of the bumble bee whose numbers are on the decline. I didn't have a bee costume as theirs had been prepared sometime before but I did have a black and white mini skirt which I matched with a black strappy top which, when put together was sort of bee-like. I met my fellow bees at a house owned by one of the girls where costumes were being assembled. I helped them to get their costumes together and then Mindy gave me a spare set of wings that she had made, together with a black mask and some stick on antennas. All in all I thought that I looked the part. Mindy, who is a very talented mixologist, had a tray fixed to her bee costume with some cocktail glasses glued to it and called herself the 'barbee', very funny!

We met up with the rest of the people at the rendezvous point which was the cemetery in the centre of town. There were thousands of people in fantastic costumes with varying themes. One that made me laugh was a few guys dressed in Mexican sombreros and ponchos. They had an imitation brick wall which they were carrying in front of them with some references to the newly elected president. All along the route there were people watching the parade and having a good time, together with lots of camera crews and even a news helicopter overhead. With so many people taking part progress was very slow with frequent stops along the way. Some of the hotels had put out tables filled with free cocktails and at one point I met Dave Bootle who was there with his lovely wife Marie and a pitcher filled with his own 'bootle bomb' cocktail. Don't know what went into it but it sure tasted good. The parade ended on Simonton Street and though you could have walked the route in fifteen minutes it had taken up all of the afternoon. We finished up in Bobbies Monkey Bar on Simonton for some celebratory drinks. I watched the main fantasy fest parade the next day from the bar at La Te Da and though it was undoubtedly spectacular, the locals' parade was by far the best one for me. Thanks a million Mindy.

Chapter 6

One night I was sitting in The Little Jazz Room on Duval waiting for a date. After a while it seemed obvious that I had been stood up so finishing off my chardonnay I got up to leave. At that moment a girl sat down next to me at the bar and offered to buy me another drink. I explained that I was just about to go but she insisted, her name was Sheri and we became good friends. I saw Sheri on and off on subsequent occasions and, though we always promised to have dinner together, as yet we still haven't got around to it. We do keep in touch on Facebook though when I am back in the UK. Earlier this year I wrote a short piece for 'Keys Voices' which is an online magazine, it was called 'Discovering Mandy's Key West and it was published in August. Sheri read this piece and said how much she liked it, she then told me that I should write more. That's how this story got written, thanks to Sheri, who also very kindly wrote the foreword for this book.

Let me return to the beginning with Hurricane Irma heading directly for Key West. There is a church in Key West called The Basilica of Saint Mary Star of the Sea and in the grounds of this church is a small grotto. This was built by a nun, Sister Louis Gabriel in the early part of the last century. The sister, who had been living in Key West for around twenty years had seen the devastating effects of three hurricanes which killed many people. She decided to build the grotto which depicts the appearance of the Virgin Mary in Lourdes and said that as long as the grotto stood, Key West would be spared severe devastation by a hurricane. There have been many hurricanes in the years since, including a major one in the 1930's that killed many people in Marathon in the middle keys and destroyed the overseas railroad, but strangely none of them have scored a direct hit on Key West.

With the eye of Irma predicted to make a direct hit on the island, many residents lit candles in the grotto. Make of it what you will, but with the hurricane just an hour or so away it shifted to the east and the eye missed Key West. At this point I have to say how saddened I am by what happened in the middle keys where it did hit and where many people lost their homes and their livelihoods, but once again Key West got off relatively lightly. After the power went down on that terrible night the only way that people could find out what was happening was through social media. My friend Sheri had moved the year before to the mainland (which was hit by Irma a few hours later) and she, along with all of the

Keys residents that had evacuated, was desperate for information about those that stayed. You can appreciate that, with the power down in much of the state, it was very difficult to get information but, as it did filter though, Sheri was on Facebook telling everyone what she knew. There were many people doing the same thing but I thank Sheri for keeping me informed about what was happening.

In the days that followed, the relief effort was nothing short of magnificent. The authorities had their plans in place to get food and water down to the keys and to get the power back on and did a fantastic job, but there was also a tremendous effort by many private citizens to get relief sent down as well. Supplies came in from all over the USA and, as well as government efforts, I have read of fleets of private aircraft and boats ferrying supplies down to the lower keys. I have never seen or heard of anything like it and I salute all of the brave people that put their lives on hold to help the people on those islands.

Irma struck on September 9th and caused widespread damage but, incredibly, Key West opened its doors (and bars and restaurants of course) to visitors on October 1st. There is still a lot of damage, particularly in the middle keys but Fantasy Fest will still go on at the end of October and thousands of people will watch another spectacular parade along Duval Street. The spirit of Key West and the Conch Republic is as strong as ever!

And I'll be going back home soon……..

Happy Ever After (2020)

Epilogue? Not really, more the continuing story of Mandy Murray.

The hurricane of 2017 was bad, very bad and even now, three years on, you can still see the damage in and around Big Pine where many homes were destroyed along with many trees. Sadly some people also died as a result of Irma which is considered one of the worst hurricanes in the history of the state.

The work of recovery and rebuilding went on apace and, as mentioned earlier Key West was indeed open for business for Fantasy Fest that year.

I returned to Key West in 2018 and managed to stay for seven weeks between late July and early September. This is a quiet time in the Keys, very much the off season, but I like it when the streets aren't crowded as they are in the winter. It's a very relaxing time of year but you have to be able to take the heat and high humidity. Fortunately the temperatures stay around the high 80's due to the cooling sea breezes but it does feel much hotter as it is also very humid.

My visit this year was very special as it enabled me to strengthen my friendships with the people of the island and also make new ones. This has really been a theme of my visits in recent years. One night last year at Bobbies Monkey Bar a young guy came up to me and said *"You are Mandy aren't you? I bought your book and read it, I think you are great"*.

I was very taken aback by this, this sort of thing just doesn't happen to ordinary people like me. I was so surprised that I texted my friends Nina and Sharon to tell them about it and sharon texted me back with something that amazed me even more. *"You are very well known, People are attracted to you, not just physically but you are a very kind and approachable person. Just think how many others you may have helped by just being you"*.

Now, I am not showing off here, I am mentioning this because to me it is quite remarkable that people should feel that way. When I see my friend Carter he keeps asking me why I am so nice. I don't feel any more special than the next T girl, and people in Key West are all very nice in my experience, so why do people keep saying this. All I can say is that if I do help some people along the way by being myself, then I am very happy and privileged.

When I returned in 2018 the very talented Dave Bootle (praised earlier in the book) had moved from La Te Da and was performing four nights a week at Mangoes, an open air bar / restaurant further along Duval. It therefore became a favourite place for me and I would go every night that Dave performed. As he told me (and everyone else in the place) on my last night in 2019, I had been to see him no fewer than 36 times on that trip. Some would say that is a little sad, but given that he is such a great entertainer to dance to, and I have very many friends who frequent the place, it's fine by me.

Dave also did something special for me in 2018, he changed the words of 'Brandy You're a Fine Girl' by Looking Glass to 'Mandy You're a Fine Girl'.

This has kind of stuck now and he even sings it unintentionally when asked for the song when I'm not there. On the occasions that he forgets and sings 'Brandy' a regular at the bar, my good friend Alan Alan Alan (no typo, it's his nickname), calls out "Its Mandy Bootle, not Brandy!" How cool is it to have a song re written especially for you.

As I said earlier I have made many new friends in the last couple of years and, in addition to the many friends already mentioned in this book, I would just like to thank them so, Seann and EJ, Donna, Michelle, the aforementioned Alan, Daniel, Kevin, Bruce, Sammy, Paul, Lucy, The Reverend Steve and Larry, thank you all for making me feel so very welcome. And if I have left anyone out it is unintentional and I am VERY sorry.

As an aside, Larry, who is a well-known professional photographer, is a very tall guy and one night at Mangoes he asked me to dance. He was so much taller than me that I felt like a little girl in his arms, how wonderful.

Last year I was there for the Pride celebrations at the beginning of June. A great many parties happen in Key West during Pride week and I tried to get to some of them. The Pride kick-off Party at The Island House was FAB and I had a great time there with Carter, EJ and Seann. The after parade party at La Te Da was equally fun with more people attending than they get for fantasy Fest.

You will have read how I took part in the local's parade during Fantasy Fest week in 2016. Well last year I had the opportunity to take part in another parade.

In 2019 I had decided to be in Key West for the months of May and June, 9 whole weeks!

Lots of wonderful things happened during my stay which I may tell you about later but one thing really stands out.

I had been back in KW for two weeks when I saw a piece in Konk Life asking for volunteers to help carry the rainbow flag in the Pride Parade on June 9th. Well, I was definitely up for that and immediately sent in my name to the organisers. A couple of weeks later I received an email confirming that I had been accepted and would be one of the 40 volunteers who would be carrying the flag, I was delighted!

The rainbow flag was first created by Gilbert Baker in the 1970's and, on its 25th anniversary in 2003, he created a version of it that was over a mile long, which stretched along the entire length of Duval Street from the gulf to the ocean. The aerial photos of this are sensational. The original flag had 8 colours as opposed to the ones usually seen now that only have 6.

These are:

Pink for sex, red for life, orange for healing, yellow for sunlight, green for nature, turquoise for magic, indigo for harmony and violet for spirit.

This flag was then divided up into 100 foot sections which were sent to various cities around the world with one section remaining in Key West. This was what I had the honour of helping to carry.

Pride Day arrived and I was really excited. Got myself ready, makeup, hair and a pair of denim hot pants which my friend Carter called Daisy Dukes (a reference to a 70's TV series) and booked an Uber to take me to the rendezvous at the Truman Waterfront. He dropped me at the wrong place, the Truman Amphitheatre, where a concert was taking place but I got directions from one of the guys at the gate and headed off. The original instructions were to arrive by 3.30 but when I found the place there was no one there. I started to wonder if I was in the wrong location again but after a while people started to arrive.

Over the next hour lots of floats, decorated cars and more flag carriers turned up and everyone got into position for the parade. At five o'clock we headed off with a motorcycle escort of Key West's finest. We were at the back of the parade and I found myself second in line at the front of the flag.

First off we passed through the Truman Annex, an upmarket residential area of Key West. It was then that I got an inkling of what was to come as families were standing on their porches watching the parade and when we came along they started cheering and applauding.

We then walked along Whitehead Street, along Green Street and turned the corner onto Duval. That's when it all got crazy. The streets were lined with hundreds of people, families, kids (who kept running under the flag) and guys and girls all cheering and yelling at us saying 'you guys are great', 'we love you' and 'thank you for what you are doing'. I must have high fived over 200 people as we made our way slowly along Duval

Street. I heard my name called lots of times but I couldn't see who by in the crowd and one woman said to me 'how did you get those great legs honey?'...er, I was born with them....

By the time we got to the 800 block by the Bourbon Street pub we were brought to a stop by the mass of cheering people. By this time the rest of the parade was so far ahead that we had lost sight of them.

The love and affection that we received from the crowd was phenomenal and I have never experienced anything like it.

Finally we got to the end of the parade just past La Te Da which was packed as they were throwing a parade party. We folded the flag up and one of the organisers loaded it into his car and I headed off to La Te Da to join my friends and party the night away (but that's another story).

How did I feel about all of this? I was honoured to have been involved in carrying the flag in the parade and it was an incredible high. I would do it all again tomorrow and when I am back home at the same time this year you can bet that I will be volunteering gain.

Next I will tell you about one perfect day in Key West.

One fine day in Key West

It was a Sunday in June, it was early in the morning and it was very warm with clear blue skies. I had been invited to a birthday party a week or so before where I had met a lady who asked me if I was religious. I said that yes, I was, sort of, so she told me that I should pay a visit to the Metropolitan Community Church of Key West as they welcome all, particularly members of the LGBT community. I must admit to having been a bit nervous about whether or not I would be welcome but I promised to give it a try.

As it happened, purely by chance, I met the Pastor of the church, the Reverend Steve Torrence, a week or so later at La Te Da at the after Pride party. We had chatted a bit and I had told him about my book so this made me all the more relaxed on the day.

I woke to an early alarm call (not a normal activity after a Saturday night partying to Dave Bootle at Mangoes) as I needed a bit of time to get ready and do my makeup. I chose a modest white skirt and blue top thinking that this was appropriate for church and called an uber, as I wanted to arrive refreshed, not after a long walk in the already high heat of the day.

I walked up the steps of the beautiful building in Petronia Street and into the foyer where who should be waiting to greet people but Reverend Steve himself. He gave me a big welcome and then hit me with a BIG surprise, he had bought my book and wanted me to autograph it for him!!! How about that!

Having told him that I would be delighted to do so I walked up the stairs to the church hall and joined the congregation. Just about everyone in the room came over to introduce themselves and welcome me to their church, proving once again that Key West is the most friendly place in the world.

During the service Reverend Steve gave his sermon. I am not a regular church goer but I have to say that his was the best sermon I have ever heard. He is so very funny but at the same time sends a strong message which gives a lot of food for thought. After the service I joined some of the congregation on the deck at the rear of the church for coffee and happily signed the Reverend's book.

I left to walk into town but, walking along the sidewalk I felt so uplifted and at peace. What a wonderful experience. I was heading to the Saint Hotel where I had arranged to meet my good friends Carter and Bill for brunch. When I arrived, there was a spare seat at the bar so I took it to wait for my friends. Paul (a really great guy) was behind the bar and asked me if I wanted a mimosa. I said that in my opinion orange juice ruined the taste of good champagne so Paul, star that he is, filled my glass with the undiluted stuff! They were serving bottomless fizz and as I found out that day, it definitely was! Not only did it keep coming throughout the brunch but it was the real stuff all the way from France!

Shortly after Carter and Bill arrived together with a couple of friends so we grabbed a table and checked out the food. It was a wonderful couple of hours of great conversation, good food and great friends in a fab hotel.

Sometime early that afternoon, not too sure of the time as things had started to get a bit hazy due to the bottomless champagne, I decided that I needed to go home to freshen up my makeup and recharge my batteries as I had promised to meet my friends at the tea dance at La Te Da later on. So, as I had enjoyed the bottomless drinks rather a lot I called for an uber and headed back to the condo.

After a couple of hours to recover I changed into my dancing clothes and headed for La Te Da. The Sunday tea dance is a regular event that is well worth attending. The two bars and restaurant deck are given over to drinking, dancing and socialising (same as usual really) with great music provided by DJ Rude Girl. The whole event lasts for around 2 – 2 ½ hours and it's great fun.

The last half hour is given over to some of the great pop songs, one of which that gets played a lot, Dancing Queen, is my favourite and signature tune. On this occasion I was standing at the inside bar chatting with Tonto when my song came on. Anyone who knows me will know that when I hear this I just have to dance and this was no exception. I went mad on the dance floor and looking around me I saw lots of people having a great time, so I yelled out at the top of my voice 'what a great crowd of happy smiling people'. I got a few cheers for that.

As the dance finished we all set out for dinner at La Trattoria, a favourite restaurant on Duval. I found myself walking along one side of the street with Carter and Kevin Taylor, another good friend, with Bill and a couple of guys walking on the other side. We managed to lose sight of each other so as we passed the Tavern In The Town Carter suggested that we stop off for a drink. We went in and Carter introduced me to some of his friends who were there as 'his future ex-wife', (I hope Bill isn't reading this ☹)

Moving on we made it to 'La Trat' where we met up again with the others and had some great food at the bar with Tiffany looking after us. At one point Kevin reached over and grabbed my tits and someone took a photo. Alcohol is to blame for lots of things…..

Then Carter suggested that we all go to Bobbie's Monkey Bar, Key West's most famous karaoke bar, very popular with locals. Bobbie's stays open until 4 am so it's a great place to finish up the evening, providing that you don't have to get up in the morning…..

Now, it's true to say that I don't have a good voice. My only attempt at karaoke some years before on the Spanish island of Menorca earned me the name of 'La Gata', but Carter didn't know (or care) about that.

Unknown to me he put my name forward to the MC with a request for the song 'Mandy' by Barry Manilow and when they called my name out I had no choice but to climb on the stage. Apologising to the audience before I began I sang, to the best of my ability, the song with my name on it. I think the crowd felt sorry for me as some of them actually cheered and applauded so I didn't kill Carter after all.

At around 3 am I decided that I needed to get to bed (to sleep of course!) and headed home. After all I had had a very early start.

So, from church to monkey bar, via The Saint, a Tea Dance (with alcohol), a proposal (sort of) and dinner at little Italy. Not a bad day at all, in fact it was ……

…..one fine day in Key West! And there will be many more………….

Mandy x

If you want to contact me you are welcome to e mail me at:

mandymurray10@yahoo.co.uk

Printed in Great Britain
by Amazon